W9-BWG-309

STICKMEN'S GUIDE TO YOUR GURGLING GUTS

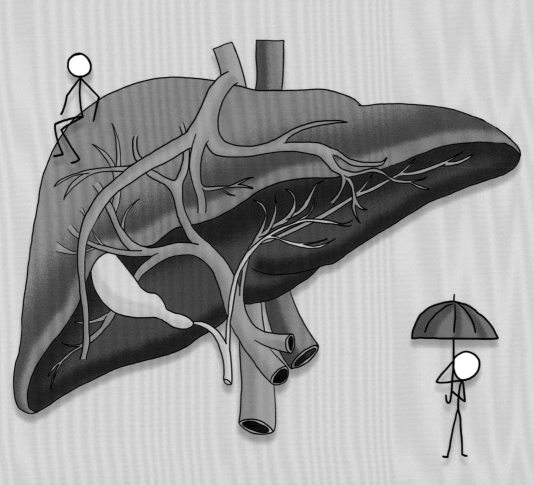

Thanks to the creative team:
Senior Editor: Alice Peebles
Fact Checking: Kate Mitchell
Design: www.collaborate.agency

Original edition copyright 2017 by Hungry Tomato Ltd.

Hungry Tomato®
A division of Lerner Publishing Group, Inc.
241 First Avenue North
Minneapolis, MN 55401 USA

For reading levels and more information, look up this title at www.lernerbooks.com.

Main body text set in Avenir Next Medium 9.5/12.
Typeface provided by Linotype AG.

Library of Congress Cataloging-in-Publication Data

Names: Farndon, John. | Dean, Venitia, 1976- illustrator.
Title: Stickmen's guide to your gurgling guts / John Farndon ; illustrated by Venitia Dean.
Description: Minneapolis : Hungry Tomato, [2018] | Series: Stickmen's guides to your awesome body | Audience: Age 8-12. | Audience: Grade 4 to 6. | Includes index.
Identifiers: LCCN 2016046944 (print) | LCCN 2016047203 (ebook) | ISBN 9781512432121 (lb : alk. paper) | ISBN 9781512450132 (eb pdf)
Subjects: LCSH: Digestion—Juvenile literature. | Digestive organs—Juvenile literature.
Classification: LCC QP145 .F37 2018 (print) | LCC QP145 (ebook) | DDC 612.3—dc23

LC record available at https://lccn.loc.gov/2016046944

Manufactured in the United States of America
1-41767-23528-1/12/2017

STICKMEN'S GUIDE TO YOUR GURGLING GUTS

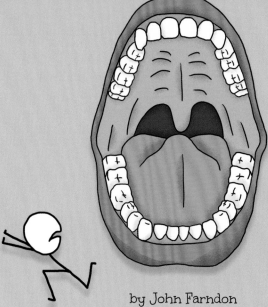

by John Farndon
Illustrated by Venitia Dean

HUNGRY TOMATO®

Minneapolis

Your stomach contains acid as strong as car battery acid—it can actually dissolve metal and bone!

Contents

Introduction

Eating gives you a constant supply of fuel and materials that keep your body going. But food comes in big lumps. That's where your digestive system plays its part. Your digestive system is an amazing chemical refinery that breaks down food into the chemicals your body needs. Then it absorbs them all into your blood for distribution around the body.

The Big Meal

Every year, the average person in the United States eats about 0.55 tons (0.5 metric tons) of food. Typically, Americans eat over 75 pounds (34 kilograms) of red meat (beef, veal, pork, and lamb) and 54 pounds (24 kg) of poultry (chicken and turkey). So altogether Americans eat nearly 20 million tons (18 million metric tons) of meat every year! That's about 160 billion quarter-pounder burgers! If all the red meat eaten by Americans each year were cows, they could form a continuous line of cattle stretching nose to tail all the way from New York City to Los Angeles, California, and back nine times!

New York

Los Angeles

2,449 miles (3,941 kilometers)

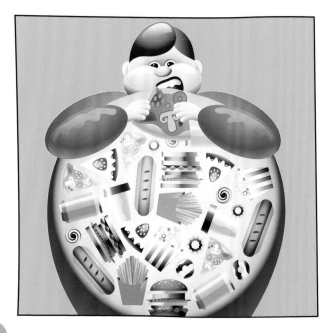

Fed Up

In the last fifty years, more and more people have been eating too much or doing too little exercise. So far more people are overweight than ever before. The World Health Organization describes those who are extremely overweight as obese, and they say that 1 billion or so people around the world are obese. Obesity can cause health problems such as heart disease and diabetes.

Cooking!

Humans are the only animals that cook their food. We cannot really digest much raw meat, so cooking softens it and allows us to eat and digest nearly any kind of meat. Meat contains a lot of protein, and some scientists think discovering how to make it edible by cooking is what gave humans such clever brains.

Basic Foods

Although we eat a far greater range of food than most other animals, we rely on a small range of simple, basic foods known as staples. These include maize, wheat, and rice, and they are crucial for giving us vital energy. Amazingly, just fifteen food plants provide 90 percent of the energy needs of the whole world.

Fast Work

While no one can live more than a few days without water, people can survive weeks, or even longer, without food. The famous Indian leader Mahatma Gandhi managed to survive twenty-one days without food. But going without food or living only on poor quality food can make you sick.

Body Fuel

Food is the fuel that keeps your body going. It also provides the materials your body needs to grow and stay in good repair. Some animals eat only meat. Others eat mostly plants. But we humans eat a wide range of foods—and to stay healthy, we need to get the right balance of ingredients from different foods.

Carbs

Carbohydrates are the number one energy fuel. They are different kinds of sugar and starch, made from big molecules of carbon, hydrogen, and oxygen. They are converted in your body into glucose that the cells use for fuel, or they're stored temporarily in your liver and muscles as glycogen.

Pasta

Spaghetti

Rice

Protein Power

Proteins make up pretty much everything in your body. They are built from different combinations of twenty amino acids. Your body can make twelve of these itself, but it needs to get the others from food to repair cells and make new ones.

Oil

Fat Stuff

Fats are the greasy parts of food that won't dissolve in water. They are sometime known as lipids. Some are solid, like cheese and meat fat. Others are liquid, like olive oil. Like carbs, fats are used for energy, but your body stores them for future use rather than using them right away.

Peanut Butter

Quantity vs. Quality

People around the world eat 2,870 calories of food a day, on average. In the United States, people eat 3,640 calories, including a high proportion of sugar, fat, and dairy products.

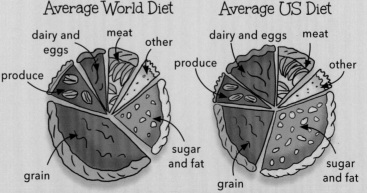

Average World Diet

dairy and eggs
meat
other
produce
sugar and fat
grain

Average US Diet

dairy and eggs
meat
produce
other
grain
sugar and fat

Vital Elements

By far the bulkiest item in your diet is carbs. But you also need tiny traces of chemicals called vitamins that your body cannot make for itself. Vitamins are known by letters A to K, and each has its own role. For example, Vitamin D is vital for healthy bones, and Vitamin A helps cell growth. Each is found in particular foods.

Mineral Essentials

Your body needs certain other minerals too. Salts maintain the right levels of water and help the nerves to work. You need calcium for building bones and iron to make red blood cells. You also need iodine and potassium, and a range of other chemicals in small amounts.

Rough Stuff

Cellulose is the tough fiber in plants that your gut can't break down. But even though you can't digest them, your body still needs this fiber, called roughage. It exercises the muscles of your gut wall and keeps them fit.

Energy-rich

Scientists measure the energy that things use in units called kilojoules or calories. An average person would use about 7,000 kilojoules or 1,700 calories of energy just sitting still for 24 hours. But when you exercise hard, your energy consumption may double.

Calorie Consumption

1,000 calories	370 calories	100 calories

14-mile (22 km) walk	climbing stairs (30 mins)	swimming (15 mins)

Throwaway

Your body carefully takes in every last useful substance from food. But a lot of food is wasted before it even gets to your mouth. About one-third of all food produced around the world is thrown away each year. If just a quarter of the food wasted were saved, it would feed 870 million hungry people!

Eating

Food provides most of what your body needs, from energy sources to building materials. But food is rarely in just the right form. So every time you eat, an amazing chemical processing factory gets to work inside you. This is what your digestive system does, and it's much more elaborate than you might think.

Mouth Power

The processing of food begins as soon as food pops into your mouth. Your teeth crush the food and break it up. Your saliva has powerful chemicals called enzymes, including one called amylase, which soften the food. Together, chewing and saliva reduce your food to a soft pulp.

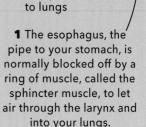

larynx

to lungs

1 The esophagus, the pipe to your stomach, is normally blocked off by a ring of muscle, called the sphincter muscle, to let air through the larynx and into your lungs.

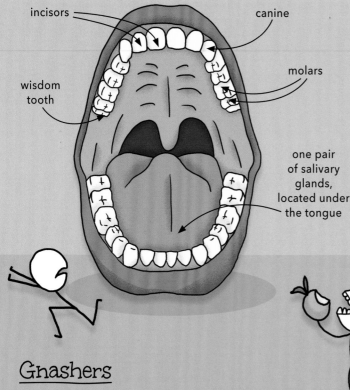

incisors

canine

wisdom tooth

molars

one pair of salivary glands, located under the tongue

Gnashers

For their size, the jaw muscles are the most powerful in the body. They can bring your teeth together with enormous force. Although you don't have the biting power of a shark, you can still give a nasty nip.

Down It Goes

Your teeth and saliva reduce food to a pulpy ball called a bolus, ready for you to swallow. But of course your throat is also the passage to your lungs. So the food in your mouth must go straight to your stomach so that it doesn't choke you!

epiglottis dropped down

bolus

sphincter muscle relaxed

epiglottis up

sphincter muscle contracted again

3 Once the bolus is in the esophagus, the larynx drops and the epiglottis opens to let you breathe again.

2 When you swallow, the top of the larynx rises out of the way, and a flap called the epiglottis shuts it off.

stomach

Sucking Up

The secret to sucking up liquid through a straw is air pressure. Your lips seal the air in the straw. To drink, you inflate your lungs. This creates a bigger space for the air in the straw and in your lungs, and lowers the air pressure. The pressure of air inside the straw is now less than the pressure of air on the drink. This pushes the drink up the straw and into your mouth.

The Food Masher

After being swallowed, food slides quickly down into your stomach. Then processing begins. Food really comes in for a rough time in your stomach! It is attacked by acids and enzymes and beaten to a pulp by squeezing muscles.

Inside the Masher

The stomach stores food and gradually lets it through to the next stage of the system. The stomach has strong, muscular walls. As soon as food enters the stomach, the muscles begin to squeeze and relax to pound and crunch the food into a soft pulp called chyme. At the same time, the food is attacked chemically by acids and the gastric juice pepsin.

The pyloric sphincter muscle opens and closes, like a rubber ring around the neck of a bag. This lets food through, bit by bit, into the small intestine.

The pylorus, or lower part of the stomach, links the stomach to the small intestine.

A sphincter muscle opens to let food from the esophagus into the stomach, then quickly closes behind it.

Muscles are in three layers to squeeze in different directions. At the top, they run lengthwise.

ring muscles

The fundus, or upper part of the stomach, holds gas that comes off the food.

diagonal muscles

duodenum, the first part of the small intestine

Inflatable Bag

When your stomach is empty, it's like a flat balloon and holds very little. But as soon as food enters, it starts swelling. How big it gets depends on how old you are. When you're born, it's no bigger than a strawberry. But by the time you're grown up, it can expand to the size of a melon!

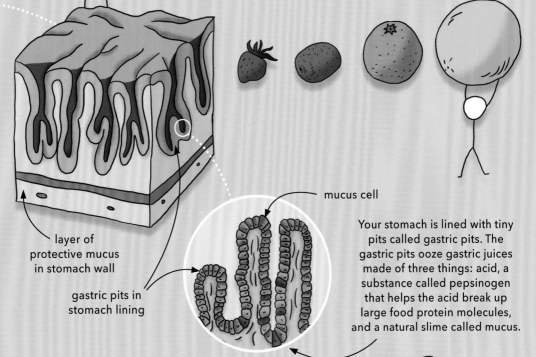

mucus cell

layer of protective mucus in stomach wall

gastric pits in stomach lining

Your stomach is lined with tiny pits called gastric pits. The gastric pits ooze gastric juices made of three things: acid, a substance called pepsinogen that helps the acid break up large food protein molecules, and a natural slime called mucus.

Acid Attack

Believe it or not, stomach acid is strong enough to dissolve metal. The acid is a mix of potassium, sodium chloride, and hydrochloric acid so powerful that it would need a safety warning if stored in a bottle. That's why the walls of your stomach must be protected by a lining of extra thick cells and a layer of slimy mucus.

It Makes You Sick

What goes down doesn't always stay down. If the vomiting center in your brain gets the message from your gut that something is wrong, it will send signals to your stomach to throw up. The muscle rings that block off your gut and the stomach suddenly open wide, and your abdomen muscles squeeze. Then up come the contents of your gut and stomach! Ugh!

Guts

After food has been turned into chyme, it moves on from your stomach into your intestines.

pancreas

duodenum: the breakdown of energy foods begins, helped by chemicals oozed from the pancreas

small intestine, a tunnel about 23 feet (7 meters) long

Small and Large Intestine

Your intestine, or gut, is divided into two sections: the narrower small intestine where food is digested and absorbed, and the wider large intestine where undigested food is dried out and prepared to exit your body. To perform all of its tasks, the gut has to be incredibly long, so it is folded over and over inside your abdomen.

large intestine or colon, where water is sucked out of waste food

ileum: more food is absorbed into the blood and swept to the liver for further processing

jejunum: food molecules seep through the gut walls into the blood

rectum, where slimy mucus helps waste to slide out through the anus

Big Gut!

The gut needs a huge area to absorb food, bit by tiny bit. So its surface area is enormous. Estimates vary, but most scientists agree that if laid out flat, it would cover an entire badminton court!

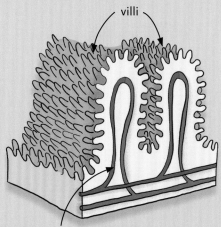

villi

blood vessels in gut wall

Foodie Fingers

Many billions of tiny food molecules have to be absorbed by the gut. So its lining is covered in millions of fingerlike projections. These are known as villi. They hugely increase the surface area of the gut, so food absorption is spread out over a vast area.

Move Along!

Food is moved through the gut by muscles in the gut wall. This process is called peristalsis. Rings of muscles just behind the chyme contract sharply, while muscles in front relax. So the chyme is eased gradually forward as muscle waves pulse along the gut.

muscle contraction

chyme

Gut Bugs

good bacteria

You might think of bacteria as germs. In fact, there is a vast community of bacteria inside your gut that helps you digest your food. These friendly bacteria break down any food that your normal digestion cannot deal with. Waste smells as it does because of the chemicals made by these bacteria snacking on food.

lactobacilli are good bacteria found in the colon

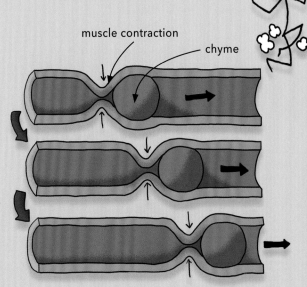

bad bacteria

The Chemical Refinery

Digestion is a complicated business. It's not just a matter of breaking food into little bits. Food also has to be sliced into tiny particles, or molecules. So the gut is an amazing chemical refinery involving acids and those chemicals called enzymes.

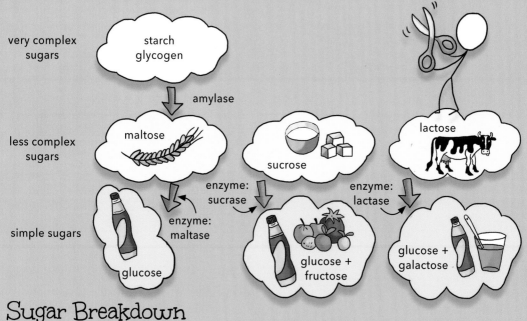

very complex sugars — starch / glycogen

amylase

less complex sugars — maltose / sucrose / lactose

simple sugars — glucose

enzyme: maltase

enzyme: sucrase — glucose + fructose

enzyme: lactase — glucose + galactose

Sugar Breakdown

The living world gets energy from chemicals called carbohydrates, including starches and sugars. They come in many forms in food, but your body can only use the simple sugar glucose. So it assigns a different enzyme to change each kind of starch into three simple sugars: glucose, fructose, and galactose. Then your liver converts fructose and galactose to glucose.

Biological Scissors

Enzymes do not break up food themselves; they just get things going. They work like biological scissors, snipping away at big food molecules, just as kitchen scissors snip at a string of sausages. For example, the enzyme amylase chops up the big starch molecules in bread and potatoes into simple sugars.

starch molecules

simple sugars

amylase

Chemical Breakdown

In the gut, muscles pound the food and open it up for clever chemical enzymes to get to work. As it passes on down, the enzymes break down the food chemically in stages.

mechanical digestion: chewing and churning

1 Amylase chops large carbohydrate molecules into simpler sugars: maltose, lactose, and sucrose.

small intestine

stomach

2 Proteins in food are broken into chains of amino acid by pepsin.

3 Amino acids are chopped up by trypsin, peptidase, and other enzymes.

4 Fats are broken up by bile from the liver and the enzyme lipase.

large intestine

6 The liver stores some glucose in the form of a sugar called glycogen.

5 The enzymes maltase, lactase, and sucrase snip the simpler sugars maltose, lactose, and sucrose into one simple sugar: glucose.

What Use is an Appendix?

Attached to the colon is a little fingerlike projection called the appendix. People once thought it was useless, and doctors simply removed it if it became infected by the disease appendicitis. Now scientists think it may be a vital safe haven for friendly gut bacteria when toxic substances sweep through.

appendix

Chemical Powerhouse

Your liver is your body's biggest internal organ, and one of its cleverest. It's a super hot powerhouse of chemical activity, generating a lot of your body's warmth and working on 500 different chemical processes at once, from purifying blood to making bile to break down fats.

gall bladder

hepatic artery

portal vein

1 Chemicals from the blood pour into the liver for processing, 24 hours a day, through two big blood vessels: the hepatic artery and the portal vein.

The Liver

The liver's most important task is to repackage the chemicals from food into just the right form for them to be used around your body. Most importantly, it keeps your blood supplied with glucose, the cells' key energy food. Guided by two chemical signals, glucagon and insulin, the liver helps make sure your blood Is always supplied with the right amount of glucose.

Liver Tasks

- ☑ Turn carbohydrates into glucose
- ☑ Store energy in the form of glycogen
- ☑ Pack away excess energy for long-term storage as fat
- ☑ Clean out old blood cells
- ☑ Make new blood plasma
- ☑ Break down waste proteins
- ☑ Turn fat into cholesterol
- ☑ Store vitamins

2 Blood vessels carry chemicals into thousands of processing units called lobules.

3 Blood flows into the lobules through pipes called sinusoids.

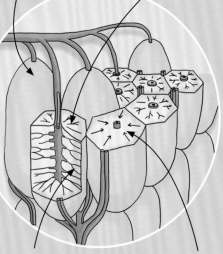

Diabetics have the insulin levels in their blood monitored to ensure the amount of sugar released by the liver stays under control.

4 Cells called hepatocytes line the sinusoids. They take out the right chemicals and process them.

5 Hepatocytes return the processed chemicals to the blood.

Blood Sugar

Your blood sugar (glucose) levels are kept steady by two chemical controls: insulin and glucagon. These are made in the pancreas, an organ just beneath your liver. When you eat, your liver makes lots of glucose and releases it into the blood. Sugar levels go up, and the pancreas oozes insulin. Insulin tells your body cells to get busy using glucose, and your liver to store more glucose as glycogen. Soon blood sugar levels drop again, and the pancreas releases glucagon, telling your liver to turn glycogen into glucose. In people who have diabetes, the control goes wrong. The diagram shows what happens.

How Diabetes Occurs

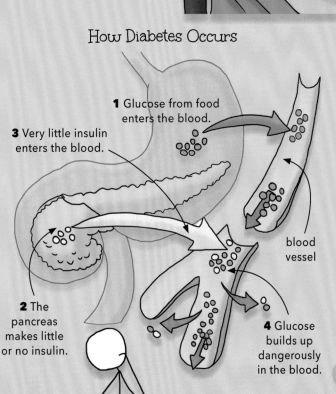

1 Glucose from food enters the blood.

3 Very little insulin enters the blood.

blood vessel

2 The pancreas makes little or no insulin.

4 Glucose builds up dangerously in the blood.

19

Warm Body

For your body processes to work, your body has to stay at exactly the same temperature all the time, whether it's hot or cold. And the body has an amazing mechanism for making sure it does just that. Unless you are sick, your body will stay at 98.6°F (37°C) all the time. Even when you're sick, your temperature only goes up by a few degrees.

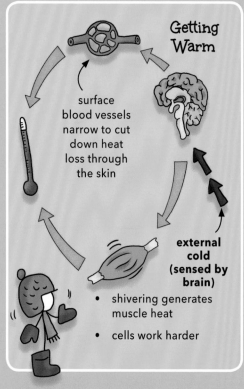

Getting Warm

surface blood vessels narrow to cut down heat loss through the skin

external cold (sensed by brain)

- shivering generates muscle heat
- cells work harder

How Do You Keep Warm?

You keep warm mainly by eating. Most of the food you eat is turned into heat by your cells—especially those in your liver and muscles. Inside every cell are little units called mitochondria which are like furnaces, releasing the energy from glucose and creating heat. All your countless mitochondria working together can make as much heat as a small electric fire!

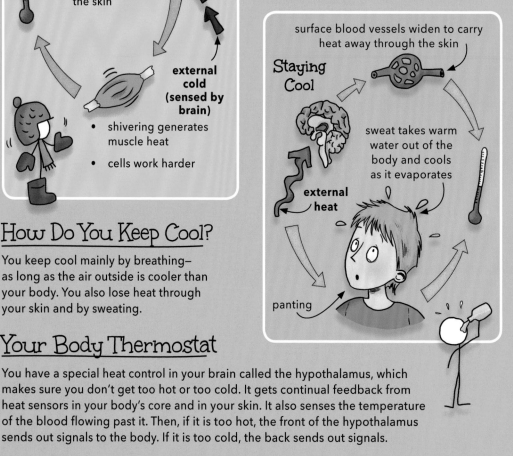

surface blood vessels widen to carry heat away through the skin

Staying Cool

sweat takes warm water out of the body and cools as it evaporates

external heat

panting

How Do You Keep Cool?

You keep cool mainly by breathing—as long as the air outside is cooler than your body. You also lose heat through your skin and by sweating.

Your Body Thermostat

You have a special heat control in your brain called the hypothalamus, which makes sure you don't get too hot or too cold. It gets continual feedback from heat sensors in your body's core and in your skin. It also senses the temperature of the blood flowing past it. Then, if it is too hot, the front of the hypothalamus sends out signals to the body. If it is too cold, the back sends out signals.

Goose Bumps

When you're cold, you may find little bumps appearing all over your arms. These are called goose bumps because they look a little like the skin of a plucked goose. If you look closely, you may see that in each, the skin hair stands erect. This may all be left over from the days of our hairier ancestors, since raising the hairs trapped warm air next to the skin.

hair   warm air on skin

muscle relaxed

cold air on skin

hair upright

love   happiness   anger   depression

muscle contracted   goose bump

Warm Heart, Cold Fish

It's sometimes said that people who are friendly are warm, and those who are unfriendly are cold. Well, that might be literally true. Scientists used special heat sensitive cameras to reveal changing body heat patterns with different moods. They found that love makes the body hot, and depression makes it cold.

Cold Extremities

Thermal image cameras confirm what you might have guessed. The coldest parts of the body are the extremities, such as the fingertips and toes. These are far away from the core of your body, which is the hottest place at all times.

If your temperature goes up a few degrees above normal, it's a clear sign that you are unwell. When you have an infection or are sick in some other way, your body may boost its temperature to help its defenses fight the germs. This is called a fever, and it can make people who are ill sweat heavily and go red. Once the fever is past and your temperature drops, it's a sign you are getting better.

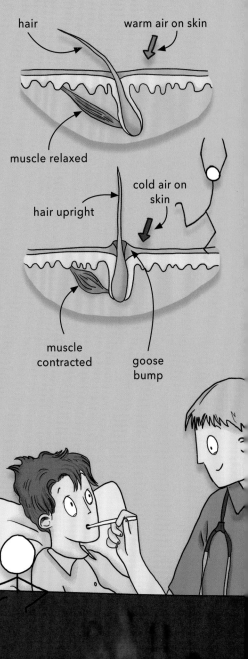

Staying Pure

Your body absolutely depends on water to work—and the key to controlling water is your kidneys. Your kidneys hold water back when needed and let it run out as urine if there is too much. They are also filters that draw any poisonous waste out of the blood.

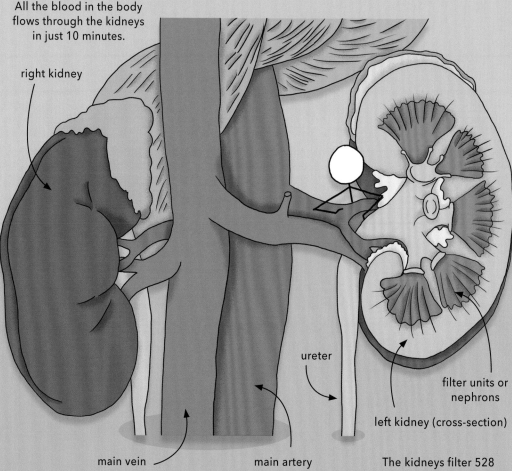

All the blood in the body flows through the kidneys in just 10 minutes.

right kidney

ureter

filter units or nephrons

left kidney (cross-section)

main vein

main artery

The kidneys filter 528 gallons (2,000 L) of blood a day. From that amount, they release only 0.4 gallons (1.5 L) of water.

Human Beans

The kidneys are a pair of bean-shaped organs in the middle of your back. They are located on the main arteries and veins, so they have easy access to the blood. Basically, their task is to clean blood as it washes through, catching larger materials and letting smaller ingredients pass on to the next stage. They then release the necessary ingredients back into the blood and let the waste and unwanted water flow away through the ureters as urine.

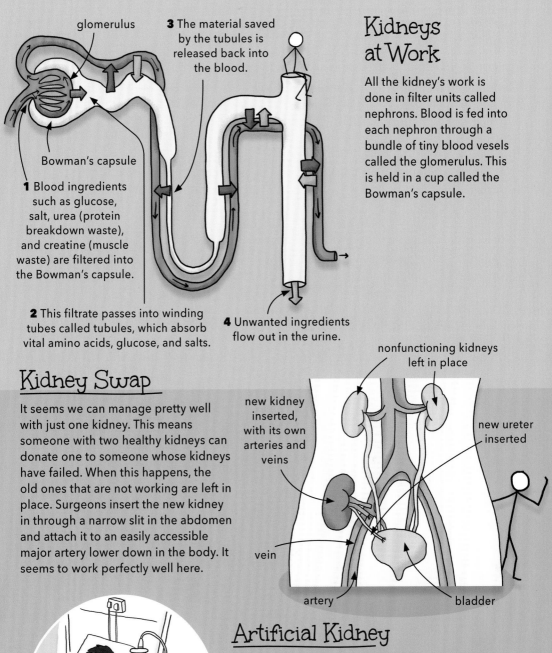

glomerulus

3 The material saved by the tubules is released back into the blood.

Kidneys at Work

All the kidney's work is done in filter units called nephrons. Blood is fed into each nephron through a bundle of tiny blood vesels called the glomerulus. This is held in a cup called the Bowman's capsule.

Bowman's capsule

1 Blood ingredients such as glucose, salt, urea (protein breakdown waste), and creatine (muscle waste) are filtered into the Bowman's capsule.

2 This filtrate passes into winding tubes called tubules, which absorb vital amino acids, glucose, and salts.

4 Unwanted ingredients flow out in the urine.

Kidney Swap

It seems we can manage pretty well with just one kidney. This means someone with two healthy kidneys can donate one to someone whose kidneys have failed. When this happens, the old ones that are not working are left in place. Surgeons insert the new kidney in through a narrow slit in the abdomen and attach it to an easily accessible major artery lower down in the body. It seems to work perfectly well here.

nonfunctioning kidneys left in place

new kidney inserted, with its own arteries and veins

new ureter inserted

vein

artery

bladder

Artificial Kidney

Many people suffer from kidney disease. A kidney transplant may solve the problem, but until a donor is found, many kidney patients have to be regularly hooked up to a dialysis machine. All the patient's blood is sent through this machine, which filters blood just as the kidneys do. It works, but it is not a comfortable experience for the patient, and it is very time-consuming.

Body of Water

You are remarkably wet. Every cell contains water, and your body fluids, such as blood, are almost entirely made up of water. Your body needs water to dissolve the chemicals that make every process happen. You can't survive for more than a day or two without water.

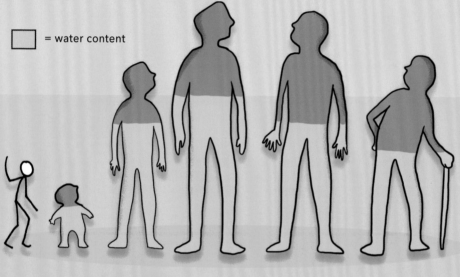

☐ = water content

Made of Water

Amazingly, babies are 86 percent water—it's almost surprising you can't hear them slosh around as they move. But they gradually dry out as they grow older. Teenagers are still about 75 percent water. Not until you're really old do you really dry out and become barely half water. It's all that water that helps people look young.

Sweating It Out

On average, you lose about 0.1 gallons (0.5 L) of water a day by sweating. Most of it quickly evaporates, so you keep dry. Only when you're hot and sweat a lot does your skin stay wet for long. You sweat more when it's hot because the evaporation helps keep you cool.

Waterworks

Your body's water content cannot change by more than 5 percent. Your urinary system—the part of your body that creates urine—plays a key role in keeping the amount of water in the body steady. You gain water by drinking and eating and as a result of cell activity. You lose it by sweating, breathing, and urinating. Your urinary system drains unwanted water.

1 Waste water is drawn off from the blood by the kidneys.

2 It trickles down the kidney's tubules into the ureter.

3 Waste water collects as urine in the bladder.

4 Pressure of urine mounts on the ring of muscle at the exit of the bladder.

5 The pressure sensors alert your brain, and you become aware of the need to urinate.

Water Balance

The amount of water your body gains each day needs to balance the water you lose. Typically, you take in about 0.58 gallons (2.2 L) to 0.4 gallons (1.4 L) in drink and 0.2 gallons (0.8 L) in food. Your body cells add an extra 0.08 gallons (0.3 L). So your body needs to lose about 0.7 gallons (2.5 L) to stay in balance. Usually your body loses 0.08 gallons (0.3 L) in your breath, 0.1 gallons (0.5 L) in sweat, 0.05 gallons (0.2 L) in feces, and 0.4 gallons (1.5 L) in urine.

Daily average water intake

body processes 10%

food 30%

fluids 60%

Daily average water output

feces 4%

sweat 8%

water vapor, etc. 28%

urine 60%

0.7 gallons (2.5 L) in and out

Waste Disposal

Your body is remarkably good at breaking down food into the bits it needs. But there are some parts of food it has no use for at all. It's the task of the last section of the digestive system, the large intestine, to deal with this unwanted waste and bundle it up for disposal.

Getting It All Out

To stay functioning well, your body needs to regularly get rid of all kinds of waste materials besides food waste. This process is called excretion, and it happens in five main ways.

Food waste from your gut is expelled as feces through the rectum.

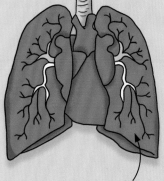

Your lungs get rid of unwanted carbon dioxide gas expelled by every cell after it uses oxygen.

Your kidneys get rid of unwanted water and dissolved chemicals in urine.

Your liver takes toxic substances out of chemicals, turning ammonia, for example, into urea.

The sweat glands in your skin help get rid of unwanted water, salts, and other dissolved chemicals.

Sewer System

The main winding part of the large intestine is the body's sewer system. It is called the colon, and its task is to convert gloopy food leftovers into feces. The colon absorbs a lot of water and salt from food waste to dry it out, helped by the bacteria that live there. In fact, a third of all feces is solid bacteria.

The colon breaks food waste into short packages.

The first part of the colon, called the ascending colon, is on your right and carries food upward.

In the process called peristalsis, the muscular walls of the colon move the packaged feces.

Peristalsis movements in the descending colon squeeze feces towards the rectum.

Besides water, the colon walls absorb sodium and chlorine and replace them with bicarbonates and potassium.

Losing Skin

Your skin is an amazing organ—protective, waterproof, and a major sensor—and it's also constantly changing and regenerating itself. So you lose 30,000 to 40,000 cells from your skin just flaking off the surface every hour. Over a day, you lose almost one million skin cells. Over a year you shed 8 pounds (3.6 kg) of skin cells. The dust that collects on your tables, TV, and other surfaces is mostly dead human skin cells! A man's skin flakes have more germs than a woman's—but a woman's have a greater variety.

The History of the Digestive System

Thinkers knew long ago that the food you eat is processed in the stomach and gut into a form the body can use, while the waste is disposed in your feces. But they didn't know just how food was processed. Some thought it was broken down mechanically. Others thought it was chemicals at work. Now we know it is both.

450 BCE

The Greek doctor Hippocrates studied digestion and decided that food was digested by being cooked inside the body by its heat. But another Greek physician, Erasistratus (around 304-250 BCE), believed digestion was a mechanical process, in which the stomach churned up food.

120 CE

The Roman doctor Galen believed that a special brew was concocted from food in the stomach. It was then absorbed into veins in the guts, and taken to the liver for making into food to distribute through the blood. He was mostly right. . . .

100 CE   **800**   **1600**

1630

The Flemish scientist Jan Baptist van Helmont did not think that food was broken up in the stomach by cooking or churning as the Greeks had suggested. He thought it was an organic process, like rotting, and involved an acid. He was right about the acid, but it involves churning too. . . .

1780

By swallowing special tubes full of food, then studying what came out the other end, Italian physiologist Lazzaro Spallanzani figured out that food did not rot in the stomach after all. Instead, it was bombarded with the acidic chemicals that we call gastric juices. He was almost right. . . .

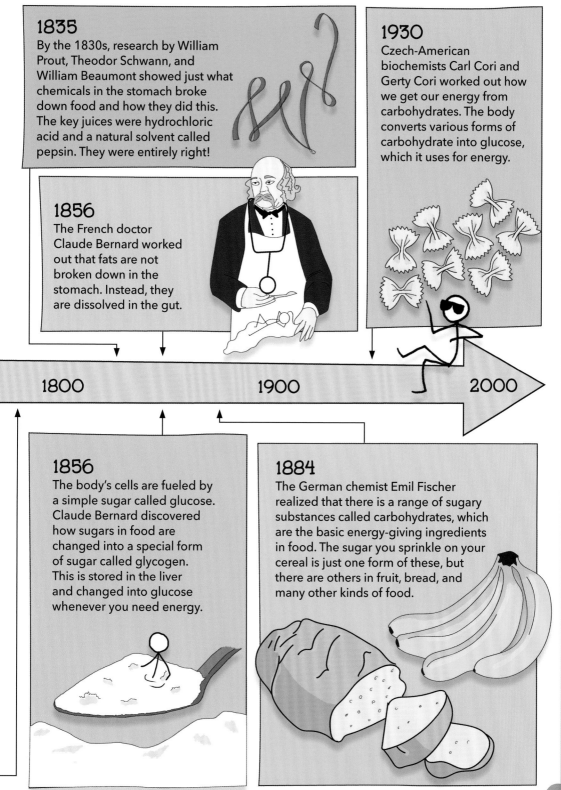

1835

By the 1830s, research by William Prout, Theodor Schwann, and William Beaumont showed just what chemicals in the stomach broke down food and how they did this. The key juices were hydrochloric acid and a natural solvent called pepsin. They were entirely right!

1856

The French doctor Claude Bernard worked out that fats are not broken down in the stomach. Instead, they are dissolved in the gut.

1930

Czech-American biochemists Carl Cori and Gerty Cori worked out how we get our energy from carbohydrates. The body converts various forms of carbohydrate into glucose, which it uses for energy.

1800   1900   2000

1856

The body's cells are fueled by a simple sugar called glucose. Claude Bernard discovered how sugars in food are changed into a special form of sugar called glycogen. This is stored in the liver and changed into glucose whenever you need energy.

1884

The German chemist Emil Fischer realized that there is a range of sugary substances called carbohydrates, which are the basic energy-giving ingredients in food. The sugar you sprinkle on your cereal is just one form of these, but there are others in fruit, bread, and many other kinds of food.

More Gutsy Facts

Fast Food

On average, food takes 24 hours to pass all the way through your guts and out the other end. Your stomach takes just 60 minutes to digest a cup of tea and a jam sandwich. Milk, eggs, and meat take more like 3–4 hours. Your stomach takes about 6–7 hours to process a big three-course meal.

The Digestion Timetable

Follow the great journey of food down through your gut:

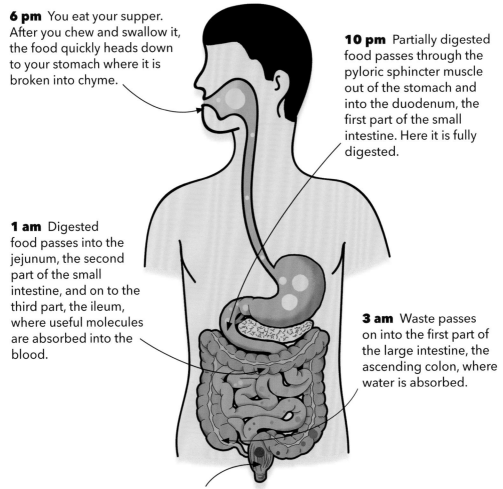

6 pm You eat your supper. After you chew and swallow it, the food quickly heads down to your stomach where it is broken into chyme.

10 pm Partially digested food passes through the pyloric sphincter muscle out of the stomach and into the duodenum, the first part of the small intestine. Here it is fully digested.

1 am Digested food passes into the jejunum, the second part of the small intestine, and on to the third part, the ileum, where useful molecules are absorbed into the blood.

3 am Waste passes on into the first part of the large intestine, the ascending colon, where water is absorbed.

11 am to 5 pm Waste passes into the rectum and is eventually excreted as feces a day or two later.

What's Urine?

Urine is 95 percent water, and about 0.4 gallons (1.5 L) is produced every day. The rest of it is, on a typical day, two tablespoons of urea, a chemical also found in saliva and body sweat; a tablespoon of salt; and some pigments, poisons, and other chemicals.

A Wee Odor

When urine is inside your body, it has no smell. The minute it comes out, however, the urea in it begins to break down and smell. The smell in stale urine is ammonia, the same chemical used in many cleaning products.

The Smell of Poop

Feces smell because of chemicals made by bacteria inside your gut. They produce smelly sulphur-containing compounds, such as indole, skatole, and thiols, as well as the stinky gas hydrogen sulphide. Undigested spices from spicy food can make feces extra smelly.

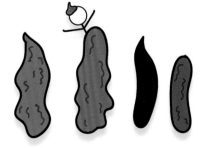

Colors of Poop

Poop is not always brown. The disease porphyria makes it purple. Prussian blue, a treatment for radiation poisoning, can color it blue. Bleeding in the gut can turn it black with old blood. Newborn babies produce green feces. Because they can't poop inside the womb, green bile digestive juice builds up.

INDEX

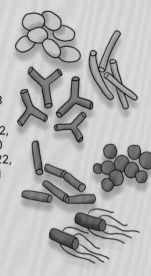

The Author

John Farndon is Royal Literary Fellow at City&Guilds in London, United Kingdom, and the author of a huge number of books for adults and children on science, technology, and nature, including such international best sellers as *Do Not Open* and *Do You Think You're Clever?*. He has been shortlisted six times for the Royal Society's Young People's Book Prize for a science book, with titles such as *How the Earth Works, What Happens When?*, and *Project Body* (2016).

The Illustrator

Venitia Dean is a freelance illustrator who grew up in Brighton, United Kingdom. She has loved drawing ever since she could hold a pencil! As a teenager she discovered a passion for figurative illustration, and when she turned nineteen she was given a digital drawing tablet for her birthday and started transferring her work to the computer. She hasn't looked back since! As well as illustration, Venitia loves reading graphic novels and walking her dog Peanut.

Picture Credits (abbreviations: t = top; b = bottom; c = center; l = left; r = right) © www.shutterstock.com:

6 tr, 6 bl, 7 tl, 7 cr, 7 bl, 15 br, 21 br.
6 bl = Bangkokhappiness / Shutterstock.com